Countries of the World

Kenya

by Michael Dahl

Reading Consultants:
J. Tepkut
E. Vodoti
Embassy of the Republic of Kenya

Bridgestone Books

an Imprint of Capstone Press

Bridgestone Books are published by Capstone Press,
151 Good Counsel Drive, P.O. Box 669, Mankato, Minnesota 56002.
www.capstonepress.com

Library of Congress Cataloging-in-Publication Data
Dahl, Michael.
    Kenya/by Michael Dahl.
    p. cm.—(Countries of the world)
    Includes bibliographical references.
    Summary: Discusses the history, landscape, people, and culture of Kenya.
    ISBN 1-56065-475-9 (hardcover)
    ISBN 0-7368-8377-0 (paperback)
    1. Kenya—Juvenile literature. [1. Kenya.] I. Title. II. Series: Countries of the world
(Mankato, Minn.)
DT433.522.D34   1997
967.62—DC21   96-50162
                                                            CIP
                                                           AC

Photo credits
Flag Research Center, 5 (left)
FPG/Osolinski, 6; Bob and Ira Spring, 8; Grehan, 18
Jean Buldain, cover, 16
Michelle Coughlan, 5 (right)
Root Resources/Kubis, 10
Unicorn/Shores, 12; Furgason, 14; Agarwal, 20

3 4 5 6 05 04 03 02 01

Table of Contents

Fast Facts 4

Maps 4

Flag 5

Currency 5

Chapter 1: The Land of Kenya 7

Chapter 2: Harambee Schools 9

Chapter 3: Roofs of Metal and Grass 11

Chapter 4: Corn, Milk, and Blood 13

Chapter 5: A Giant Zoo 15

Chapter 6: Living and Celebrating 17

Chapter 7: Nairobi 19

Chapter 8: Dancers and Jumping Contests 21

Hands On: Save Kenya's Animals 22

Learn to Speak Swahili 23

Words to Know 23

Read More 24

Useful Addresses and Internet Sites 24

Index 24

Fast Facts

Name: Republic of Kenya

Capital: Nairobi

Population: More than 28 million

Languages: Swahili and English

Religions: Roman Catholic, Protestant, Muslim

Size: 224,961 square miles (582,649 square kilometers) *Kenya is slightly smaller than the U.S. state of Texas.*

Crops: Coffee, sugarcane, and tea

Maps

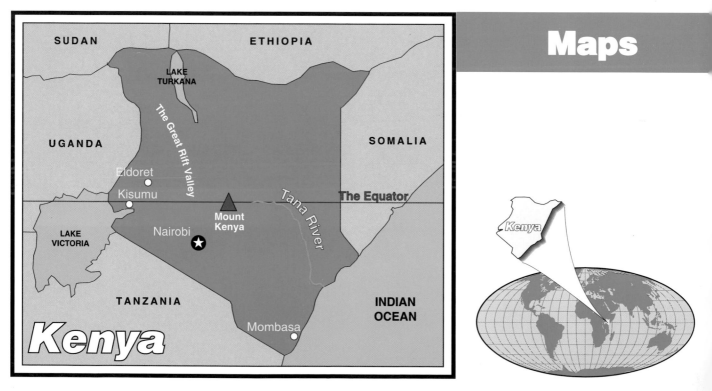

4

Flag

Kenya's flag has three different-colored horizontal stripes. The top stripe is black. The middle is red. The bottom stripe is green. The colored stripes are separated by a small white stripe. In the middle of Kenya's flag is a drawing of a warrior's shield.

Currency

Kenya's unit of currency is the Kenyan shilling.

Fifty-five Kenyan shillings equal one U.S. dollar.

The Land of Kenya

Kenya is in the middle of Africa's east coast. It is a little smaller than the U.S. state of Texas.

Water surrounds the east and west sides of Kenya. In between, it is very dry. Two short rainy seasons help farmers grow coffee and tea.

The Great Rift Valley cuts through part of Kenya. This is a huge split in the earth. Mountains rise on both sides of the split.

The equator cuts through Kenya, too. This is an imaginary line through the middle of the earth. Days are the same length all year long. The sun always shines for 12 hours.

Kenya's nickname is the cradle of mankind. Scientists found many skeletons of early humans there.

Mountains rise on the sides of the Great Rift Valley.

Harambee Schools

In Kenya, both rich cities and poor towns build their own schools. Kenyans call these harambee (HAH-rahm-bee) schools. Harambee means "let's work together."

Kenyan students are glad to attend school. They help keep the school neat. Students mow grass, pull weeds, and scrub walls. Some harambee schools have dirt floors. Students sweep the dirt floors to keep them clean.

The first eight years of school are free. After that, parents must pay for their children to attend. At all schools, students must wear uniforms.

All schools require students to wear uniforms.

Roofs of Metal and Grass

Most Kenyans live in the country. They live on farms. Some live in small villages.

Most people have huts made of grass, mud, or reeds. Usually, women build the huts from branches, cow dung, and ashes.

People in the country walk barefoot. In good weather, meals are cooked outside. At night, family members sleep together in one room. Beds are flat mats made of straw.

Lately, many Kenyans have moved into new houses with cement floors. The walls are made of concrete blocks. The roofs are metal.

Usually, women use branches to build huts.

Corn, Milk, and Blood

Corn is the main food of most Kenyans. Corn is pounded into a thick soup called uji (oo-JEE).

Ugali (oo-GAH-lee) is another common Kenyan food. It is made of white corn flour mixed with water. Ugali becomes hard like bread. It is eaten with vegetables, meat, or milk.

In the country, many people raise sheep, cattle, or goats. Cow or goat milk is a part of many meals. In some parts of Kenya, they make a special drink. It is made from sour milk and cow's blood.

Farmers in Kenya grow bananas, coffee, pineapples, oranges, and sugarcane to sell. In big cities, people eat hamburgers and pizza, too.

Many country people raise goats.

A Giant Zoo

Some of the world's best-known animals live in Kenya. Lions chase antelope over grassy fields. Hippos cool themselves in muddy rivers. Running herds of zebras kick up giant clouds of dust.

Millions of bright pink flamingos eat in Kenya's lakes. Sharp-toothed crocodiles prowl the shores. Mosquitoes in the jungles carry diseases.

Four record-holding animals live in Kenya. Elephants are the largest land animals. Cheetahs run faster than any other animal. Giraffes are the tallest animals. The ostrich is the largest bird.

Hippos cool themselves in muddy rivers.

Living and Celebrating

Many kinds of people make up the country of Kenya. The Gikuyu (geye-KOO-yoo) people are Kenya's largest group. They grow fruits, vegetables, and coffee.

The Masai (MAH-seye) people raise cattle in southern Kenya. The El Molo (EL MOH-loh) people fish and live on Lake Turkana. The Luo (LOH) and Somali (sah-MAH-lee) people raise camels, sheep, and goats.

Each of Kenya's different groups celebrates the birth of a child. The village is invited to a party for the new baby. Villagers dance, feast, and drink all day.

Every December 12, each of Kenya's different groups also celebrates Jamhuri Day. This holiday honors the day Kenya became an independent country. No one works on Jamhuri Day.

Villagers dance to celebrate the birth of a new baby.

Nairobi

Nairobi is a busy, modern city. People from around the world are moving to Nairobi. It is growing faster than any other African city.

Many people from small villages move to Nairobi to work. But sometimes there is no work. It is hard to find a place to live.

Nairobi National Park borders Nairobi. Leopards, giraffes, lions, and zebras roam the park.

Sometimes a lion or leopard escapes from the park. It sleeps in someone's backyard. In the morning, the lion gets up and leaves.

Animals eat grass in Nairobi National Park.

Dancers and Jumping Contests

Kenyans like to dance on special holidays. They dance to celebrate marriage or the birth of a child. Some dances honor the death of a villager. Sometimes dances tell stories about animals or heroes.

Soccer is the most popular sport in Kenya. Their national soccer team is called the Harambee Stars.

The Safari Rally is a famous race in Kenya. It is a dangerous car race that lasts three days. It is dangerous because cars sometimes spin out of control. Drivers or onlookers can be killed.

Masai people have their own sports events. They have contests to see who can jump the highest.

Masai people have jumping contests.

Hands On: Save Kenya's Animals

Kenya's cities and villages are growing. There is less room for wild animals. Wild animals have a harder time finding food.

Recently, thousands of rhinos have died from poaching. This is illegal hunting. Elephants are also killed illegally for their ivory tusks.

You can help protect Kenya's animals. Write to the following addresses. Ask them how you can help. Send a stamped envelope to the African Wildlife Foundation. You will need international reply coupons to put on the Rhino Anti-Poaching Operation envelope. You can purchase these at the Post Office. Remember to put your name and address on both envelopes.

Rhino Anti-Poaching Operation
IUCN
Regional Office: Eastern Africa
P.O. Box 68200
Nairobi, Kenya

African Wildlife Foundation
1400 16th Street NW
Suite 120
Washington, DC 20036

Learn to Speak Swahili

friend	rafiki	(rah-FEE-kee)
good-bye	kwaheri	(kwah-HAY-ree)
hello	jambo	(JAHM-boh)
no	la	(LAH)
sorry	samahani	(sah-ma-HAY-nee)
thanks	asante	(ah-SAHN-teh)
welcome	karibu	(kah-REE-boo)
where	wapi	(WAH-pee)
yes	naam	(nah-AHM)

Words to Know

El Molo (EL MOH-loh)—an ethnic group of people in Kenya who fish for a living

Gikuyu (geye-KOO-yoo)—an ethnic group of people in Kenya who farm for a living

Great Rift Valley (GRAYT RIFT VAL-lee)—a huge split in the earth

Luo (LOH)—an ethnic group of people in Kenya who raise camels, sheep, and goats

Masai (MAH-seye)—an ethnic group of people in Kenya who raise cattle for a living

Somali (soh-MAH-lee)—an ethnic group of people in Kenya who raise camels, sheep, and goats

uji (oo-JEE)—a thick corn soup

Read More

Derr, Victoria. *Kenya*. Milwaukee: Gareth Stevens, 1999.

Dunne, Mairead. *Kenya*. Country Insights. Austin, Texas: Raintree Steck-Vaughn, 1998.

King, David C. *Kenya: One Nation, Many Cultures*. New York: Benchmark Book, 1998.

Internet Sites

FactHound offers a safe, fun way to find Internet sites related to this book. All of the sites on FactHound have been researched by our staff.

Here's how:

1. Visit www.facthound.com
2. Type in this special code **1560654759** for age-appropriate sites. Or enter a search word related to this book for a more general search.
3. Click on the **Fetch It** button.

FactHound will fetch the best sites for you!

Index

cheetahs, 15
crocodiles, 15
El Molo, 17
elephants, 15
equator, 7
flag, 5
Gikuyu, 17

Great Rift Valley, 7
hippos, 15
hut, 11
lions, 15, 19
Luo, 17
Masai, 17, 21
Nairobi, 4, 19

ostrich, 15
Safari Rally, 21
school, 9
soccer, 21
ugali, 13
uji, 13